AL-QAEDA: THE THREAT TO THE UNITED STATES AND ITS ALLIES

HEARING

BEFORE THE

SUBCOMMITTEE ON
INTERNATIONAL TERRORISM, NONPROLIFERATION
AND HUMAN RIGHTS

OF THE

COMMITTEE ON
INTERNATIONAL RELATIONS
HOUSE OF REPRESENTATIVES

ONE HUNDRED EIGHTH CONGRESS

SECOND SESSION

APRIL 1, 2004

Serial No. 108–103

Printed for the use of the Committee on International Relations

Available via the World Wide Web: http://www.house.gov/international_relations

U.S. GOVERNMENT PRINTING OFFICE

92–869PDF   WASHINGTON : 2004

For sale by the Superintendent of Documents, U.S. Government Printing Office
Internet: bookstore.gpo.gov   Phone: toll free (866) 512–1800; DC area (202) 512–1800
Fax: (202) 512–2250   Mail: Stop SSOP, Washington, DC 20402–0001

COMMITTEE ON INTERNATIONAL RELATIONS

HENRY J. HYDE, Illinois, *Chairman*

JAMES A. LEACH, Iowa
DOUG BEREUTER, Nebraska
CHRISTOPHER H. SMITH, New Jersey,
  Vice Chairman
DAN BURTON, Indiana
ELTON GALLEGLY, California
ILEANA ROS-LEHTINEN, Florida
CASS BALLENGER, North Carolina
DANA ROHRABACHER, California
EDWARD R. ROYCE, California
PETER T. KING, New York
STEVE CHABOT, Ohio
AMO HOUGHTON, New York
JOHN M. McHUGH, New York
ROY BLUNT, Missouri
THOMAS G. TANCREDO, Colorado
RON PAUL, Texas
NICK SMITH, Michigan
JOSEPH R. PITTS, Pennsylvania
JEFF FLAKE, Arizona
JO ANN DAVIS, Virginia
MARK GREEN, Wisconsin
JERRY WELLER, Illinois
MIKE PENCE, Indiana
THADDEUS G. McCOTTER, Michigan
KATHERINE HARRIS, Florida

TOM LANTOS, California
HOWARD L. BERMAN, California
GARY L. ACKERMAN, New York
ENI F.H. FALEOMAVAEGA, American
  Samoa
DONALD M. PAYNE, New Jersey
ROBERT MENENDEZ, New Jersey
SHERROD BROWN, Ohio
BRAD SHERMAN, California
ROBERT WEXLER, Florida
ELIOT L. ENGEL, New York
WILLIAM D. DELAHUNT, Massachusetts
GREGORY W. MEEKS, New York
BARBARA LEE, California
JOSEPH CROWLEY, New York
JOSEPH M. HOEFFEL, Pennsylvania
EARL BLUMENAUER, Oregon
SHELLEY BERKLEY, Nevada
GRACE F. NAPOLITANO, California
ADAM B. SCHIFF, California
DIANE E. WATSON, California
ADAM SMITH, Washington
BETTY McCOLLUM, Minnesota
BEN CHANDLER, Kentucky

THOMAS E. MOONEY, SR., *Staff Director/General Counsel*
ROBERT R. KING, *Democratic Staff Director*

SUBCOMMITTEE ON INTERNATIONAL TERRORISM, NONPROLIFERATION
AND HUMAN RIGHTS

ELTON GALLEGLY, California, *Chairman*

CHRISTOPHER H. SMITH, New Jersey
DANA ROHRABACHER, California
PETER T. KING, New York
JOSEPH R. PITTS, Pennsylvania
MARK GREEN, Wisconsin
CASS BALLENGER, North Carolina
THOMAS G. TANCREDO, Colorado
NICK SMITH, Michigan
MIKE PENCE, Indiana

BRAD SHERMAN, California
JOSEPH CROWLEY, New York
SHELLEY BERKLEY, Nevada
GRACE NAPOLITANO, California
ADAM B. SCHIFF, California
DIANE E. WATSON, California
BETTY McCOLLUM, Minnesota

RICHARD MEREU, *Subcommittee Staff Director*
DONALD MACDONALD, *Democratic Professional Staff Member*
RENEE AUSTELL, *Professional Staff Member*
JOSEPH WINDREM, *Staff Associate*

CONTENTS

AL-QAEDA: THE THREAT TO THE UNITED STATES AND ITS ALLIES

THURSDAY, APRIL 1, 2004

House of Representatives,
Subcommittee on International Terrorism,
Nonproliferation and Human Rights,
Committee on International Relations,
Washington, DC.

The Committee met, pursuant to call, at 9:42 a.m. in Room 2172, Rayburn House Office Building, Hon. Elton Gallegly presiding.

Mr. GALLEGLY. The Subcommittee will come to order. Today, the Subcommittee on International Terrorism, Nonproliferation and Human Rights is focusing its oversight responsibility on al-Qaeda, which, by all accounts, remains the number-one terrorist threat in the United States and to its people.

On March 9th, in testimony before the Senate Armed Services Committee, CIA Director George Tenet underlined this view by warning that al-Qaeda terrorists were trying to acquire weapons of mass destruction and planning spectacular attacks against the United States and its allies. I agree that al-Qaeda continues to be a dangerous threat to all of our citizens and to our interests around the world. However, I also believe that al-Qaeda has fundamentally reorganized since September 11, 2001, and that our counterterrorism strategy needs to reflect the new al-Qaeda structure and new al-Qaeda strategy.

Since it lost its sanctuary in Afghanistan, al-Qaeda has evolved into a much more decentralized organization relying on either semi-autonomous cells or affiliated groups to carry out its deadly plans. Recent attacks bear out this strategy. The May 16, 2003, suicide attacks in Casablanca that killed 45 people were carried out by attackers belonging to a local terrorist group who were recruited and trained by al-Qaeda.

In the November 2003 suicide bomb attack in Istanbul that killed 25 people and wounded more than 300, the group that claimed responsibility, Abu Haps Al Masiri Brigades, is linked to al-Qaeda. A few days later, an attack against a bank and British consulate in Istanbul has been tied to another local terrorist group with ties to al-Qaeda.

Lastly, the preliminary results of the investigation into the Madrid bombings point to the involvement of Moroccan Islamic radicals who were members of the Al Sala Haljatayah, all organizations affiliated with al-Qaeda.

These four attacks were executed by four different terrorist groups. However, each of these four organizations are connected, either through recruitment and training of Afghanistan or localist help, all tied to al-Qaeda. They demonstrate that al-Qaeda can inflict major casualties with smaller physical infrastructure and more decentralized operations. Although we must still guard against a large-scale, planned attack by Osama bin Laden or other senior al-Qaeda leaders, the United States must respond to the threat posed by al-Qaeda-affiliated organizations.

On a related matter, I would like to also explore the extent to which al-Qaeda is not only an organization but has also become an ideology. Has it spawned completely independent groups or individuals who are bent on killing Americans or citizens with pro-American countries, and are we doing enough to isolate al-Qaeda and discredit the radical ideology of bin Laden as part of a long-term strategy to defeat this terrorist organization?

I would like to now recognize the gentleman from California, Mr. Sherman, for the purposes of an opening statement, and I just want to check. Were you going to yield your time to Mr. Schiff, or did you want to take the time?

Mr. SHERMAN. What I would like to do is yield ¾ of the time to Mr. Schiff. Why do not I yield 3 minutes to the gentleman from Burbank?

Mr. GALLEGLY. Very good. The gentleman from Burbank, Mr. Schiff.

Mr. SCHIFF. Mr. Chairman, I want to thank you, and, Ranking Member Sherman, I want to thank you for generously loaning me some of your time.

For millions of Americans, last week's hearings of the 9/11 Commission were an opportunity to revisit the horror of September 11th. Now, 2½ years after the attacks, we are able to look back at 9/11 and the months that preceded it and ask ourselves what, if anything, we could have done to prevent the calamity that morning. This is properly a job for the 10 commissioners, and I trust that their report will be comprehensive and fair but also unsparing. The murder of 2,996 people demands nothing less.

Nevertheless, I would like to offer some thoughts on the conduct of the government in the years leading up to 9/11, for it is a cautionary tale that should guide all of us in thinking about the war on terrorism. I reject those on either side of the aisle who have sought to exploit the attacks for political gain, but that does not mean that we can shrink from fulfilling our duty to exercise oversight of the conduct of the Executive Branch.

The commission and the joint congressional intelligence panel that investigated the terrorist attacks in 2002 have focused on a multitude of systemic and bureaucratic failures that crippled our ability to piece together the disparate bits of information that the intelligence and law enforcement communities were receiving in the spring and summer of 2001. However, I believe that the root of the problem was a combination of an inability or a refusal to imagine that attacks such as those that occurred on September 11th were possible. It was a world view that did not view nonstate actors as urgent threats to our national security.

The testimony before the 9/11 Commission, the report of the joint intelligence panel, and numerous media accounts have painted a fairly clear picture of some of our policies toward al-Qaeda, and I think that, at the sum of these, we know that in the summer and spring of 2001 American intelligence was picking up an incredibly high volume of information that suggested that al-Qaeda was planning a major attack against the United States. However, the danger posed by al-Qaeda did not fit the threat paradigm that framed our view of the world.

Our failure to stop 9/11, if such a thing was even possible, was not a result of bad intelligence or ill will by officials of one Administration or those of another; it was, I think, a failure to imagine that such a thing was even possible. The need to imagine, to try to separate ourselves from the world view that guides our response to threats and information about possible threats, is especially important now.

The al-Qaeda of today is different from the al-Qaeda of 2001. Like a virus, al-Qaeda has evolved and adapted to the U.S.-led war against it. Already diffused, it has become less an organization than a banner. Whereas 15 of the 19 9/11 hijackers were Saudis, the majority of those arrested in the wake of the Madrid train station attacks were Moroccans. Two days ago, British Security Services arrested eight suspected terrorists and seized half a ton of ammonium nitrate fertilizer. Those arrested were Islamic extremists, but all had been born and raised in Britain. British officials said that the eight had no known connection to the al-Qaeda hierarchy, but can there be any doubt that they were inspired by Osama bin Laden?

President Bush has said that the struggle against al-Qaeda will be a long one. I agree with him. I also agree with Richard Clarke, who said that al-Qaeda has come to resemble a mythic hydra, where one head is lopped off, two more emerge from the bloody neck. We may have made remarkable inroads in destroying the al-Qaeda of 2001, but my question for Ambassador Black is this: Are we making progress against the al-Qaeda of 2004?

Again, I thank the Chair and Ranking Member for their indulgence, and I look forward to hearing from our witness.

Mr. GALLEGLY. Mr. Sherman.

Mr. SHERMAN. Thank you. It is said that there is nothing that we could have done. The fact is that after the East Africa bombings, after the Cole, or upon the inauguration of the new Administration, we could have initiated the very policies that we adopted in the fall of 2001, and we would have been justified in doing so. In the fall of 2001, we took action which so far has prevented al-Qaeda, with, I might add, some good luck on our part, from carrying out an attack here in the United States.

I want to contrast what we did with Afghanistan for harboring al-Qaeda, on the one hand, and our approach toward Iran. Iran harbors at least three major al-Qaeda figures. They acknowledge it. They say these folks are in custody. I guess Club Med could be "in custody." They say they will put them on trial. So far, that has not happened.

I draw attention to the Big Three of al-Qaeda in Iran: Bin Laden's son, Sayeed, who is, of course, a Saudi citizen; Sayeef Al Adel, the operative most likely to have masterminded the planning of the May 2003 Riyadh bombings, and he probably did that while he was in Iran. He is an Egyptian. Then there is Sulaman Abdu

Gaysi, a self-styled spokesman for al-Qaeda who is a Kuwaiti national. There are others.

Afghanistan harbored al-Qaeda. We invaded. Iran harbors al-Qaeda. We give the green light to Japan to send Iran $2.8 billion in oil investments. We ignore the Iran-Libyan Sanction Act or use all of the outs and waivers in it. We try to bring international attention to Iran's nuclear program, but we have used up so much of the world's goodwill by how we have dealt with Iraq. And then, finally, we import $150 million of caviar and carpets from Iran, and we do that because even the slightest inconvenience of our business is not something we are willing to do to bring pressure on a nation that is harboring al-Qaeda, major figures, including one of bin Laden's sons, and is building nuclear weapons to someday smuggle them into the American cities. I yield back.

Mr. GALLEGLY. I thank the gentleman.

I would like to welcome Ambassador Cofer Black today. Ambassador Black serves as Ambassador-at-Large and coordinator for counterterrorism at the State Department.

The Department of State is the lead Federal agency dealing with international terrorism. On behalf of the secretary, Ambassador Black represents the department for the Counterterrorism Security Group. His office plays a leading role on the Department of State's Counterterrorism Task Forces organized to coordinate responses to the international terrorist incidents. Ambassador Black's responsibilities include coordinating U.S. Government efforts to improve counterterrorism cooperation with foreign governments, including the policy and planning of the department's Antiterrorism Training Assistance program.

Prior to his State Department appointment, Ambassador Black served for 28 years in the Directorate of Operations at the CIA, including as the director of the CIA Counterterrorism Center.

Welcome this morning, Ambassador Black.

STATEMENT OF THE HONORABLE J. COFER BLACK, AMBASSADOR-AT-LARGE, COORDINATOR FOR COUNTERTERRORISM, U.S. DEPARTMENT OF STATE

Mr. BLACK. Thank you very much, Mr. Chairman and distinguished Members of the Subcommittee. Thank you for the opportunity to testify today on the evolving nature of the al-Qaeda organization and the continuing threat that it presents the United States and our allies.

This hearing provides a welcome opportunity to bring you and your colleagues up to date on this threat. I will also describe the steps we are taking to defeat the al-Qaeda organization.

As the State Department's coordinator for counterterrorism, I have been charged with managing the U.S. Government's international efforts to counter terrorism through the coordination of our efforts with those of our allies. It is precisely this sort of coordinated action that has scored some important successes against the al-Qaeda organization.

Just over 2½ years ago, our nation suffered a devastating attack on its own soil, a day that none of us will forget. Since that terrible day of September 11, 2001, we have undergone a transformation as a nation and have fully engaged in a war with terrorism. The

President's vision and message for the world has been crystal clear: Any person, organization, or government that supports, protects, or harbors terrorists is complicit in the murder of the innocent and will be held to account.

We are carrying out the President's clear directive and our taking the fight to the terrorists worldwide using all of the elements of national power. We are also enlisting the support of friends and allies in the international community to great effect. We have made great progress in marshalling the collective strength of the international community into the counterterrorism fight, but we must continue to press forward to face and to defeat terrorism.

Although there are numerous terrorist organizations of concern in the world today, the top priority of our efforts has been on the al-Qaeda organization, its affiliates, and those who support them. Al-Qaeda remains a potent force, despite the continuing efforts of the community of civilized nations to remove this evil from the world. Al-Qaeda is determined to strike the United States, our allies, and interests wherever it can, using the most destructive means at its disposal. Mr. Chairman, I have no doubt whatsoever that al-Qaeda would use unconventional weapons if it possessed the capability to do so.

Since the Coalition's successful ouster of the Taliban from al-Qaeda, the al-Qaeda organization has been deeply wounded. It has been forced to evolve in ways not entirely of its own choosing. However, it remains determined to murder Americans, whether overseas or in our own country. Al-Qaeda has amply shown its willingness to kill and maim large numbers of innocent civilians around the world, regardless of faith, nationality, race, class, and creed.

Regarding the Madrid attack, the tragic events of 11 March in Madrid show the potent global terrorist threat. We continue to see mounting evidence of al-Qaeda links to the attacks, although we are still awaiting the conclusions of the ongoing investigation by the Spanish government.

The Spanish government is uncovering evidence of linkages between suspects in custody and the perpetrators of the 16 May 2003 Casablanca bombings. Time and Spain's progress in its investigations will tell us about the extent of al-Qaeda's involvement, particularly its senior leadership.

One lesson from the Madrid bombings is clear. We have learned this lesson before in the streets of Istanbul, Riyadh, Casablanca, Bali, Moscow, and Mombassa: No country is safe from the scourge of terrorism. No country is immune from attack, and neither policies of deterrence nor accommodation will ward off attack. Al-Qaeda seeks only death and chaos, which is why we will continue to pursue the only viable course of action before us, which is to destroy this enemy utterly, both with the cooperation of our allies and by unilateral action when necessary.

The removal of the Taliban regime from Afghanistan stripped al-Qaeda of its primary sanctuary and support and shut down long-standing terrorist training camps. Although our work continues in Afghanistan to root out the remnants of al-Qaeda's former strength, al-Qaeda has lost a vital safe haven. With the loss of Afghanistan and its terrorism infrastructure there, al-Qaeda has been separated from facilities central to its chem-bio and poisons development programs.

We and our coalition of partners have also removed the regime of Saddam Hussein in Iraq, a longtime sponsor of terror. The al-Qaeda-affiliated Zarqawi network continues to spread terror and death as the Iraqi people move toward a brighter future free from the tyranny of Saddam Hussein.

Iraq is currently serving as a focal point for the foreign jihadist fighters, who are united in a common goal with former regime elements, criminals, and more established foreign-terrorist organizations to conduct attacks against Coalition and Iraqi civilian targets. These jihadists view Iraq as a new training ground to build their extremist credentials and hone the skills of the terrorist. We are aggressively rooting out foreign fighters in Iraq and will continue to devote the resources necessary to ensure that al-Qaeda and other terrorist groups will be unable to use Iraq as a training ground or sanctuary.

We have relied on the support of our partners in the global coalition against terrorism to ensure al-Qaeda is unable to establish a new secure base of operations like that which existed under the Taliban Afghanistan. The partnership of Saudi Arabia, Pakistan, Yemen, and others has been, and will continue to be, essential to ensuring that al-Qaeda is never able to reestablish comfortable sanctuary anywhere in the world.

Historically, al-Qaeda has been a top-down organization with strong central leadership control over almost all aspects of its operations. However, our ongoing operations against al-Qaeda have served to isolate its leadership and sever or complicate communications links with its operatives scattered around the globe. Unable to find easy sanctuary in Afghanistan and elsewhere, the al-Qaeda leadership must now devote much more time to evading capture or worse.

This has further complicated al-Qaeda's communications and co-ordination efforts, which are much harder and time consuming in the current operating environment. We have also seen examples of terrorist activities delayed for extended periods as al-Qaeda affiliates await instructions from an increasingly isolated central leadership.

Also, as al-Qaeda's known senior leadership, planners, facilitators, and operators are brought to justice, a new cadre of leaders is being forced to step up. These individuals are increasingly no longer from the old guard, no longer the seasoned, veteran, al-Qaeda trainers from Afghanistan's camps or close associates of al-Qaeda's founding members.

Critical gaps have been cut out of the al-Qaeda leadership structure. These relatively untested terrorists are assuming greater responsibilities, and we are relentlessly going after these new leaders are they are identified.

This confluence of factors may be resulting in a lack of clear strategic direction and operational mistakes by al-Qaeda. An example is the 8 November 2003 bombing of the Muhaya housing complex in Riyadh which killed 18 persons, predominantly Muslims, during the month of Ramadan. This target selection, made either by mistake or due to poor judgment, was a public relations disaster for al-Qaeda, which, in turn, has assisted aggressive Saudi efforts to role up the al-Qaeda presence in the kingdom. Whether this operation was plagued by operational or strategic error is still a matter of debate, but I believe that it is indicative of the complications faced by al-Qaeda in its truncated organization.

A few words, if I may, now about al-Qaeda's influence. I know I am going a bit past my 5 minutes. If I may, I think it is useful, Mr. Chairman,—I am talking as fast as I can—to get this out to frame your questions because I am trying to preempt some of the questions I know you would like to ask.

Mr. GALLEGLY. I appreciate that, and it is my error for not catching. I wanted to give you a little more time to start with.

Mr. BLACK. I appreciate it very much. I hope this is useful to your Committee. I have tried to hit some of the high points that you are interested in to facilitate your questions.

I would like to talk a little bit about al-Qaeda's influence having spread to other organizations. There are growing indications that a number of largely Sunni Islamic extremist groups are moving to pick up al-Qaeda's standard and attempting to pursue global jihad against the United States or our allies.

There are also growing indications that al-Qaeda's ideology is spreading well beyond the Middle East, particularly its virulent, anti-American rhetoric. This has been picked up by a number of Islamist extremist movements which exist around the globe. This greatly complicates our task in stamping out al-Qaeda and poses a threat in its own right for the foreseeable future.

Literally, scores of such groups are present around the world today. Some groups have gravitated to al-Qaeda in recent years, where before such linkages did not exist. This has been at times merely an effort to gain greater public renown for their group or cause, but more troubling have been the groups seeking to push forward al-Qaeda's agenda of worldwide terror.

In particular, groups like Ansar al-Islam and the Zarqawi network post a real threat to U.S. interests. This has been shown very clearly by their deadly activities in Iraq. We have all seen the newspapers today, Mr. Chairman, and we see how that is most unfortunate, and our hearts go out to the relatives of those that have been lost in the struggle but particularly today in such a horrific way. Other groups of great concern include the Salafist Group for Call and Combat (GSPC), which operates mainly in the countries of North Africa, and Salifiya Jihadia, which claimed responsibility for the May 2003 Casablanca bombings. Jemaah Islamiya (JI) and the Islamic Movement of Uzbeckistan (IMU) should also be on our short list.

While it would be a mistake to believe that we are now confronted by a monolithic threat posed by legions of like-minded terrorist groups working in concert against our interests, it would be fair to say that we are seeing greater cooperation between al-Qaeda and smaller Islamic groups, as well as even more localized organizations. I think this last point is important.

Identifying and acting against the leadership, capabilities, and operational plans of these groups poses a serious challenge now and for years to come.

In addition to these groups, there are literally thousands of jihadists around the world who have fought in the conflicts of Kosovo, Kashmir, Chechnya, and elsewhere. As I said earlier, we see these "foreign fighters" operating in Iraq, where we are fighting them on a daily basis with the Coalition and Iraqi partners. These jihadists will continue to serve as a ready source of recruits for al-Qaeda and other affiliated organizations.

A Strategy To Defeat Terrorism. Let me go back for a moment to frame the overall strategy that we have been employing to defeat terrorism. Following the 11 September attacks, we have forcefully applied the Bush doctrine: Any person or government that supports, protects, or harbors terrorists is complicit in the murder of the innocent and will be held to account. We have done so through our national strategy to combat terrorism, which creates the policy framework for coordinated actions to prevent terrorist attacks against the United States, its citizens, its interests, and its friends around the world and, ultimately, to create an international environment inhospitable to terrorists and all those who support them.

We have implemented this strategy to act simultaneously on four fronts: First, defeat terrorist organizations of global reach by attacking their sanctuaries, leadership, finances, and command, control, and communications; next, deny further sponsorship, support, and sanctuary to terrorists by cooperating with other states to take action against these international threats; also, to reduce the underlying conditions that terrorists seek to exploit by enlisting the international community to focus its efforts and resources on the areas most at risk; also, to defend the United States by using our national strategy, employing all of the element of national power, diplomatic, financial, law enforcement, intelligence, and military.

While the United States is committed to combating terrorism the world over in whatever form it takes to threaten the American people and American interests, the focus of our efforts since September has been on the al-Qaeda organization. I would like to tell you a little bit about the progress that we have made.

A global dragnet has tightened around al-Qaeda, made possible by a broad coalition of 84 nations, all focused on the common goal of eradicating the terrorist threat that endangers all civilized nations. Since 11 September 2001, 70 percent of al-Qaeda senior leadership and more than 3,400 lower-level al-Qaeda operatives or associates have been detained or killed in over 100 countries, largely as a result of cooperation among law enforcement and intelligence agencies. Terrorist cells have been wrapped up in nations in all corners of the globe, from Singapore to Italy and Saudi Arabia, as well as here at home in Buffalo, Portland, and North Carolina.

A growing list of senior al-Qaeda associates have been removed from the scene and no longer threaten the United States, such as Khalid Sheikh Mohammad, Hambali, Nashiri, who ran al-Qaeda operations in the Saudi Arabian peninsula; Abu Ali al-Harithi, Abu Assem al-Makki, and the rest.

The al-Qaeda figures we take out of circulation perform roles in all operational areas, including finance, logistics, training, and procurement, among others. This has sapped al-Qaeda's strength by disrupting its ability to coordinate complex operational plans and gather operatives, materials, and funding required to carry them out.

We have also made extensive progress in the area of finances. More than 172 countries have issued orders freezing of seizing approximately $200 million in terrorism-related financial assets.

In addition to attacking known accounts, more than 100 countries worldwide have introduced new terrorist-related legislation and regulations, including new laws to block money laundering. We have an effective program that keeps track of terrorist organizations. We have a designation process, Mr. Chairman, and I thank you and your Committee for the helpful work you have done to move this along to save us time. I am very grateful, and I would appreciate your continued efforts in that area. The more time we save in one area, we can devote in others doing good works.

Meanwhile, we have also strengthened our defenses here at home, including a comprehensive reorganization of our government to better protect the homeland, and we have implemented many procedures in this area. In terms of the State Department, we have enhanced areas such as the Anti-Terrorism Assistance Training Program, our Terrorist Interdiction Program, and the like. Again, the support from Congress has been instrumental, and we are very grateful for it.

This is definitely a long-term fight. This is a war. This is a fight. I wish I could bring you some good news, it was all going to be concluded shortly and positively. I think the qualities required for this are determination, as is reflected in the encouragements that come from our leadership.

In conclusion, I would like to stress that while we have made substantial progress toward eradicating the threat posed by al-Qaeda, we are on a long, tough road. We cannot afford to falter, Mr. Chairman. The one lesson I have learned in counterterrorism is that weakness is exploited, and it must not be shown.

The al-Qaeda organization has been gravely wounded and forced to evolve in new ways to survive. However, al-Qaeda is a patient, resourceful, and flexible organization, and it is able to draw on the global support of jihadists around the world. It must be denied safe haven. It has got to be kept on the run while we starve it of resources, dismantle its cells, and apprehend its foot soldiers at our borders. We do have advantages we are exploiting. We must more than match its flexibility and resolve and commit to combat al-Qaeda for the long haul and eliminate this evil.

As President Bush recently said:

> "The war on terror is not a figure of speech. It is an inescapable calling of our generation. . . . There can be no separate peace with the terrorist enemy. Any sign of weakness or retreat simply validates terrorist violence and invites more violence for all nations. The only certain way to protect our people is by early, united, and decisive action."

I think I will stop at this point. I have greatly exceeded my time. I am very grateful for that, but perhaps I have, if not answered some of your questions, helped to frame some of your questions. Thank you.

[The prepared statement of Mr. Black follows:]

PREPARED STATEMENT OF THE HONORABLE J. COFER BLACK, AMBASSADOR-AT-LARGE, COORDINATOR FOR COUNTERTERRORISM, U.S. DEPARTMENT OF STATE

Mr. Chairman, Distinguished Members of the Subcommittee, thank you for the opportunity to testify today on the evolving nature of the al-Qaida organization and the continuing threat that it presents to the United States and our allies. This hearing provides a welcome opportunity to bring you and your colleagues up to date on this dangerous threat. I also will describe the steps we are taking to defeat the al-Qaida organization.

As the State Department's Coordinator for Counterterrorism, I have been charged with managing the U.S. Government's international efforts to counter terrorism through the coordination of our efforts with those of our allies. It is precisely this sort of coordinated action that has scored some important successes against the al-Qaida organization.

Just over two and a half years ago, our nation suffered a devastating attack on its own soil, a day that none of us will forget. Since that terrible day of September 11, 2001, we have undergone a transformation as a nation, and have been fully engaged in a war with terrorism. The President's vision and message for the world has been crystal clear: Any person, organization, or government that supports, protects, or harbors terrorists is complicit in the murder of the innocent, and will be held to account.

We are carrying out the President's clear directive, and are taking the battle to terrorists worldwide using all the elements of national power. We are also enlisting the support of friends and allies in the international community, to great effect. We have made great progress in marshalling the collective strength of the international community into the counterterrorism fight, but we must continue to press forward to face and defeat terrorism.

Although there are numerous terrorist organizations of concern in the world today, the top priority of our efforts has been on the al-Qaida organization, its affiliates and those who support them. Al-Qaida remains a potent force, despite the continuing efforts of the community of civilized nations to remove this evil from the world. Al-Qaida is determined to strike the United States, our allies and interests wherever it can, using the most destructive means at its disposal. I have no doubt that al-Qaida would use unconventional weapons if it possessed the capability to do so.

Since the Coalition's successful ouster of the Taliban regime from Afghanistan, the al-Qaida organization has been deeply wounded. It has been forced to evolve in ways not entirely by its own choosing. However, it remains bent on murdering Americans, whether overseas or in our own country. Al-Qaida has amply demonstrated its willingness to kill and maim large numbers of innocent civilians around the world, regardless of faith, nationality race, class and creed.

THE MADRID ATTACK

The tragic events of 11 March in Madrid demonstrate the potent global terrorist threat. We continue to see mounting evidence of al-Qaida's links to the attacks, although we are still awaiting the conclusions of the ongoing investigation by the Spanish government.

The Spanish government is uncovering evidence of linkages between suspects in custody and the perpetrators of the 16 May 2003 Casablanca bombings. Time and Spain's progress in its investigation will tell us about the extent of al-Qaida's involvement, particularly its senior leadership.

One lesson from the Madrid bombings is clear. We have learned this lesson before on the streets of Istanbul, Riyadh, Casablanca, Bali, Moscow and Mombassa: No country is safe from the scourge of terrorism. No country is immune from attack, and neither demographics nor policies of deterrence or accommodation will ward off attack. Al-Qaida seeks only death and chaos, which is why we will continue to pursue the only viable course of action before us: to destroy this enemy utterly, both with the cooperation of our allies and by unilateral action when necessary.

SANCTUARY LOST

The removal of the Taliban regime from Afghanistan stripped al-Qaida of its primary sanctuary and support, and shut down long-standing terrorist training camps. Although our work continues in Afghanistan to root-out the remnants of al-Qaida's former strength, al-Qaida has lost a vital safe haven. With the loss of Afghanistan and its terrorism infrastructure there, al-Qaida has also been separated from facilities central to its chem-bio and poisons development programs.

We and our coalition partners have also removed the regime of Saddam Hussein in Iraq, a long-time state sponsor of terror. The al-Qaida-affiliated Zarqawi network continues to spread terror and death as the Iraqi people move towards a brighter future free from the tyranny of Saddam Hussein.

Iraq is currently serving as a focal point for foreign jihadist fighters, who are united in a common goal with former regime elements, criminals and more established foreign terrorist organization members to conduct attacks against Coalition and Iraqi civilian targets. These jihadists view Iraq as a new training ground to build their extremist credentials and hone the skills of the terrorist. We are aggressively rooting out the foreign fighters in Iraq, and we will continue to devote the resources necessary to ensure that al-Qaida and other terrorist groups will be unable to use Iraq as a training ground or sanctuary.

We have relied on the support of our partners in the global coalition against terrorism to ensure that al-Qaida is unable to establish a new secure base of operations like that which existed under the Taliban in Afghanistan. The partnership of Saudi Arabia, Pakistan, Yemen and others has been, and will continue to be, essential to ensuring that al-Qaida is never able to reestablish comfortable sanctuary anywhere in the world.

THE STATE OF AL-QAIDA LEADERSHIP

Historically, al-Qaida has been a top-down organization with strong central leadership control over almost all aspects of its operations. However, our ongoing operations against al-Qaida have served to isolate its leadership, and sever or complicate communications links with its operatives scattered around the globe. Unable to find easy sanctuary in Afghanistan and elsewhere, the al-Qaida leadership must now devote much more time to evading capture or worse.

This has further complicated al-Qaida's communication and coordination efforts, which are much harder and time-consuming in the current operating environment. We have also seen examples of terrorist activities delayed for extended periods as al-Qaida affiliates await instructions from an increasingly isolated central leadership.

Also, as al-Qaida's known senior leadership, planners, facilitators and operators are brought to justice, a new cadre of leaders is being forced to step up. These individuals are increasingly no longer drawn from the old guard, no longer the seasoned veteran al-Qaida trainers from Afghanistan's camps or close associates of al-Qaida's founding members.

Critical gaps have been cut out of the al-Qaida leadership structure, and these relatively untested terrorists are assuming far greater responsibilities. We are relentlessly going after these new leaders as they are identified.

This confluence of factors may be resulting in a lack of clear strategic direction and operational mistakes by al-Qaida. An example is the November 8, 2003 bombing of the Muhaya housing compound in Riyadh which killed 18 persons, predominantly Muslims during the month of Ramadan. This target selection, made either by mistake or due to poor judgment, was a public relations disaster for al-Qaida, which in turn has assisted aggressive Saudi efforts to roll-up the al-Qaida presence in the Kingdom. Whether this operation was plagued by operational or strategic error is still a matter of debate, but I believe that it is indicative of the complications faced by al-Qaida in its truncated and besieged state.

ALLIES IN SOWING TERROR

A few words now on how al-Qaida's influence has spread to other terrorist organizations. There are growing indications that a number of largely Sunni Islamic extremist groups are moving to pick up al-Qaida's standard and attempting to pursue global jihad against the United States and our allies.

There are also growing indications that al-Qaida's ideology is spreading well beyond the Middle East, particularly its virulent anti-American rhetoric. This has been picked up by a number of Islamic extremist movements which exist around the globe. This greatly complicates our task in stamping out al-Qaida, and poses a threat in its own right for the foreseeable future.

Literally scores of such groups are present around the world today. Some groups have gravitated to al-Qaida in recent years, where before such linkages did not exist. This has been, at times, merely an effort to gain greater public renown for their group or cause, but more troubling have been the groups seeking to push forward al-Qaida's agenda of worldwide terror.

In particular, groups like Ansar al-Islam and the Zarqawi network pose a real threat to U.S. interests. This has been demonstrated very clearly by their deadly activities in Iraq. Other groups of great concern include the Salafist Group for Call and Combat (GSPC), which operates mainly in the countries of North Africa and Salifiya Jihadia, which claimed responsibility for the May 2003 Casablanca bombings. Jemaah Islamiya (JI) and the Islamic Movement of Uzbeckistan (IMU) should also be on this short list.

While it would be a mistake to believe that we are now confronted by a monolithic threat posed by legions of like-minded terrorist groups working in concert against our interests, it would be fair to say that we are seeing greater cooperation between al-Qaida and smaller Islamic extremist groups, as well as even more localized organizations.

Identifying and acting against the leadership, capabilities and operational plans of these groups poses a serious challenge now and for years to come.

In addition to these groups, there are literally thousands of jihadists around the world who have fought in conflicts in Kosovo, Kashmir, Chechnya and elsewhere. As I said earlier, we see these "foreign fighters" operating in Iraq, where we are fighting them on a daily basis with the Coalition and Iraqi partners. These jihadists will continue to serve as a ready source of recruits for al-Qaida and other affiliated terrorist groups.

A STRATEGY TO DEFEAT TERRORISM

Let me go back for a moment to frame the overall strategy we have been employing to defeat terrorism.

Following the September 11 attacks, we have forcefully applied the Bush doctrine: any person or government that supports, protects, or harbors terrorists is complicit in the murder of the innocent, and will be held to account. We have done so through our National Strategy to Combat Terrorism, which creates the policy framework for coordinated actions to prevent terrorist attacks against the United States, its citizens, its interests and its friends around the world and, ultimately, to create an international environment inhospitable to terrorists and all those who support them. We have implemented this strategy to act simultaneously on four fronts:

- Defeat terrorist organizations of global reach by attacking their sanctuaries, leadership, finances, and command, control and communications;
- Deny further sponsorship, support, and sanctuary to terrorists by cooperating with other states to take action against these international threats;
- Diminish the underlying conditions that terrorists seek to exploit by enlisting the international community to focus its efforts and resources on the areas most at risk; and
- Defend the United States, its citizens and interests at home and abroad. The National Strategy highlights that success will only come through the sustained, steadfast, and systematic application of all elements of national power—diplomatic, financial, law enforcement, intelligence, and military.

While the United States is committed to combating terrorism the world over, in whatever form it takes to threaten the American people and American interests, the focus of our efforts since September has been on the al-Qaida organization. Let me tell you about the progress we have made, and how the al-Qaida organization looks far different than it did in September 2001.

U.S. ACCOMPLISHMENTS, AL-QAIDA LOSSES

A global dragnet has tightened around al-Qaida, made possible by a broad coalition of 84 nations, all focused on the common goal of eradicating the terrorist threat that endangers all civilized nations. Since September 11, 2001, 70 percent of al-Qaida senior leadership and more than 3,400 lower-level al-Qaida operatives or associates have been detained or killed in over 100 countries, largely as a result of cooperation among law enforcement and intelligence agencies. Terrorist cells have been wrapped up in nations in all corners of the globe, from Singapore to Italy and Saudi Arabia, as well as here at home in Buffalo, Portland, and North Carolina.

A growing list of senior al-Qaida leaders and associates will no longer threaten the United States and our allies:

- Al-Qaida operations chief Khalid Sheikh Mohammad,
- Senior planner for Southeast Asia Hambali,
- Persian Gulf operations chief Nashiri and his suspected successor Khaled Ali al-Haj,
- Yemen's most senior al-Qaida figures Abu Ali al-Harithi and Abu Assem al-Makki.

The al-Qaida figures we take out of circulation performed roles in all operational areas, including financing, logistics, training and procurement, among others. This has sapped al-Qaida's strength by disrupting its ability to coordinate complex operational plans and gather the operatives, materials and funding required to carry them out.

We have made extensive efforts to attack al-Qaida's financing, which is the life-blood of its murderous activities, providing for the movement of operatives, the co-option of officials and local populations, and the acquisition of arms and explosives. More than 172 countries have issued orders freezing or seizing approximately $200 million in terrorism-related financial assets and accounts.

In addition to attacking known accounts, more than 100 countries worldwide have introduced new terrorist-related legislation or regulations, including new laws to block money-laundering and the misuse of charities in the support of terrorists.

An important tool in countering terrorism financing is the authority the Secretary of State uses to formally designate Foreign Terrorist Organizations. This authority, under the AntiTerrorism and Effective Death Penalty Act of 1996 freezes a designated group's assets in the United States, makes it a criminal offense for Americans to provide funding and other forms of material support and denies visas to members of the designated group. Thirty-six groups are currently designated.

Mr. Chairman, I would like to express our appreciation to you and your staff for your sponsorship of the pending legislation to make the provision even stronger by making it easier to designate an alias of group if it adopts a new name and to simplify the time consuming review of the designations every two years. This will allow us to focus our resources on the legal documents needed to designate new groups, such as offshoots of al-Qaida, when they emerge.

Meanwhile, we have strengthened our defenses here at home, including a comprehesive reorganization of our government to better protect the homeland. We have also implemented more stringent screening measures, and engaged with our international community to raise global standards. For example, in Africa, we and our colleagues in the Departments of Transportation and Homeland Security are implementing a program to secure airports in countries where the danger to aviation is particularly striking (Safe Skies for Africa).

We must also continue to provide frontline countries the training and assistance needed to support their counterterrorism efforts. The Department of State's Anti-Terrorism Training Assistance (ATA) Program, Terrorist Interdiction Program (TIP) and other counterterrorism training are vital parts of this effort.

The support of the Congress for this and other capacity-building programs will be essential to eradicating al-Qaida and other terrorist groups. Many of our most important successes have come through joint or unilateral actions by foreign governments. Improving the counterterrorism capacity of key states is clearly in our interest. While the dividends of such investment may not be immediately apparent, we must think of our global war on terrorism as a long-term fight that will take years or, indeed, decades, as was the case with the Cold War.

CONCLUSION

In conclusion, I should stress that while we have made substantial progress toward eradicating the threat posed by al-Qaida, we are on a long, tough road, and we cannot afford to falter.

The al-Qaida organization has been gravely wounded, and forced to evolve in new ways to survive. However, al-Qaida is a patient, resourceful and flexible organization and is able to draw from a global support base of jihadists and international mujahedin movement. It must be denied safe haven and kept on the run, while we starve it of its resources, dismantle its cells, and apprehend its foot soldiers at our borders. We must more than match its flexibility and resolve, and commit to combat al-Qaida over the long haul, for there can be no accommodation with this evil.

As President Bush recently said, "The war on terror is not a figure of speech. It is an inescapable calling of our generation. . ..There can be no separate peace with the terrorist enemy. Any sign of weakness or retreat simply validates terrorist violence, and invites more violence for all nations. The only certain way to protect our people is by early, united, and decisive action."

Our continued dedication to the eradication of al-Qaida with the support of our international partners is the only way to ensure the elimination of the threat posed by al-Qaida. The fates of the civilized nations of the world are inextricably linked— we must face this fight together and eradicate the al-Qaida scourge from the face of the Earth.

Thank you again for the opportunity to appear before you. I would be happy to take your questions.

Mr. GALLEGLY. Thank you, Mr. Ambassador. I am just a little concerned. We may have a vote here shortly, so I will try to make my initial questions brief, and we will get down the line so everyone gets a fair opportunity.

Mr. Ambassador, as far as you can discuss in open session, what is al-Qaeda's current operational capabilities to plan and carry out a 9/11-style attack compared to its capability prior to 9/11?

Mr. BLACK. Again, I will try to be as forthcoming as I can within the context that this is an open hearing, the results of which are broadcast around the world, including to my enemies, so with that in mind, I will be as helpful as I can.

First of all, I have been at this for quite a while. I like to think I know what I am talking about. The al-Qaeda organization that we engaged before 9/11 and at 9/11 has been put under catastrophic stress. Seventy percent of their leadership has been arrested, detained, or killed. The majority of the rest of them are essentially primarily defensive, concerned primarily about their own personal security. There is a massive global hunt for them underway. It is relentless, 24 hours a day. So despite that, they do try and plan operations. They attempt to communicate with each other to lend coherence to their organization.

So the al-Qaeda of old: Catastrophic stress; comprehensive, successful engagement; and heading toward complete destruction. The bad news is that, realizing that their capabilities are greatly reduced, they are reaching out, trying to co-opt the missions of other terrorist groups, particularly local ones and others, and try and cement their determination and their operational profile to their objectives, which is to destroy the United States, to impose their brand of Islam certainly in the Saudi Arabian peninsula and throughout the world.

So greatly reduced, greatly reduced, but the men and women who are the practitioners of counterterrorism are mindful that until all of them are accounted for, there is a threat. We know from the past that they have actively sought weapons of mass destruction, that they have been, according to our best estimates, unable to put together all of these things at one time—the people, the equipment— to launch an attack. That does not mean that this will continue.

We have to always assume the worst and conduct ourselves operationally with law enforcement, intelligence. I just heard someone from the intelligence community the other day say that regardless of who minute or minuscule the information related to weapons of mass destruction, it is hunted down to the bitter end. There is no margin for error in these things.

So I think we can say that we have been very successful to date. You are not completely successful until you close out the threat. That will be very difficult to do, but it will be the result of a long and successful struggle.

Mr. GALLEGLY. Keeping in mind how you described the diminution of their operation as a result of our effort to eliminate the threat, would it be fair to assess the threat today to that of maybe a cornered animal that is more likely to do an aggressive attack rather than the historic, calculating and methodical planning? And one follow-up question: Since 9/11, how has the recruiting gone internationally with al-Qaeda?

Mr. BLACK. To try to encapsulate an answer to what is a very hard question, the main difference is the loss of expertise and personnel in the al-Qaeda organization, per se, of today. They are left with far fewer people that know how to do these things effectively, securely. They have franchised out so that their personnel are probably of a lower standard in terms of training and expertise.

They have a greater issue with successfully planning an operation over time. They want to conduct, as in the period of 9/11, they want to conduct mass-casualties attacks; they want to kill as many people as they possibly can. They have had to degrade in a lot of their operations to operations that have less impact, that are easier to conduct. They have made fundamental operational mistakes, as I said in my testimony. They are likely to continue to do that. And in this new era, in this new time, where the old organization has been engaged and is heading toward complete destruction, and as the affiliates, the answer to your second question, the affiliates, those who have instinctive commonality with the objectives of al-Qaeda, those who watch television, those who access the Internet and gain inspiration from that, need also to be identified through intelligence/law enforcement means and engaged.

There is an advantage for us and the community of nations resisting these guys, and most of them tend to side toward—being beginners, and beginners make a lot of mistakes.

Mr. GALLEGLY. Thank you. Mr. Sherman?

Mr. SHERMAN. Al-Qaeda killed 3,000 of us. They were hoping at that time that they had killed well over 10,000. Timothy McVeigh proved that you do not have to be a rocket scientist to kill 200 Americans. In fact, the very techniques he used could be used right now.

Has al-Qaeda not engaged in an attack that would result in 100 or 200 or 300 American deaths on our soil because they are unable to, they do not even have a Timothy McVeigh capacity, or because they are unwilling to because they have set such a high standard for themselves that they do not want to cheapen their brand name by engaging in something less spectacular?

Mr. BLACK. Sure. The problem that they have encountered is lack of capability. They have more than enough will and determination.

Mr. SHERMAN. We know that they have the will and determination, if they had the capacity, to do another huge attack.

Mr. BLACK. Correct.

Mr. SHERMAN. Are you saying they lack the capacity to fill a Ryder truck filled with fertilizer and park it in an apartment building in my district? Do they lack that capacity, or are they simply unwilling to engage in such banal and unspectacular attacks?

Mr. BLACK. I think the decision-making process, the ability to process operational activity, is increasingly difficult for them. It is a challenge for them to conduct this type of attack.

Mr. SHERMAN. When you say "this type of attack,"——

Mr. BLACK. I am saying it is not easy. That is what I am saying.

Mr. SHERMAN. Even a Timothy McVeigh, two guys in a Ryder truck and a bunch of fertilizer, even the sophistication shown by a couple of guys; al-Qaeda does not have that level of operational capacity in the United States.

Mr. BLACK. I would say that, under the current, very aggressive law enforcement action, the procedures that have been taken as the result of the establishment of the Department of Homeland Security—what I am trying to convey is it is harder than it was before.

Mr. SHERMAN. We know that.

Mr. BLACK. I am just trying to make an operational point here, Congressman. I am saying there are challenges involved to maintain operational security, to accumulate all of this stuff, to have a casing plan of a target that is reflective and something that they can move against. So I am saying, if they could do it, they would do it.

Mr. SHERMAN. So you are saying, if they could kill 150 Americans the way Timothy McVeigh did, they would. The fact that they have not is not because they do not want to engage in that level of attack; it is because they cannot engage in the level of attack.

I will move on to another question. This one, I just want you to respond for the record. You told us that if al-Qaeda was harbored by a nation, that the full power and accountability of the United States would be brought to bear. Bringing in carpets and caviar or acquiescing to a $2.8 billion investment, waiving the Iran-Libya Sanctions Act; I wonder which of these are the retribution that we have imposed upon Iran for harboring the three al-Qaeda well-knowns, not to mention the others. It is absolutely shocking that we continue, for no reason except the taste for caviar, as far as I can figure, to import caviar and carpets from Iran.

They did not hit us on September 11th until they got all of their ducks in a row. They even killed a major figure in Northern Afghanistan and made sure that went well, thus, in their own minds, depriving us of the easiest methodology for getting back at them. We got back at them in Afghanistan anyway but without the charismatic leader that they assassinated.

If we had adopted right after the Cole was hit the same policy that we adopted after September 11th, would al-Qaeda have gone forward, that is to say, if we were threatening the Taliban in November and December 2000, if we were invading Afghanistan in January or February 2000, would al-Qaeda have gone forward with September 11th, and would they have been able to do so?

Mr. BLACK. I do not know, Congressman.

Mr. SHERMAN. So it could have saved us. We do not know.

Mr. BLACK. I cannot speculate. I do not know what would or would not have happened under those circumstances.

Mr. SHERMAN. Well, this is, I think, the first time the Administration has said that there was anything that could have been done a year before September 11th that might have prevented it, and I believe my time has expired.

Mr. GALLEGLY. Mr. Rohrabacher?

Mr. ROHRABACHER. Thank you very much.

Mr. Black, I would like to ask you a few questions, just to get a good understanding of the background on this. I am not going to ask you to speculate, as the last question was, but maybe just to get some details about what is going on on the inside of the government that permitted this tragedy to happen on 9/11, and what has happened since then to make sure that that has been corrected. After September 11th, what became of the State Department and the CIA officers, but especially the State Department, who insisted that, before that date, we be cooperating and working with moderate Taliban elements. Are they still in decision-making positions in the State Department?

Mr. BLACK. I have to admit, I am not too sure.

Mr. ROHRABACHER. You are right there.

Mr. BLACK. I do not know how to respond to the question.

Mr. ROHRABACHER. Well, listen, you have a long history in terms of terrorism and this whole issue.

Mr. BLACK. And I am happy to answer questions about terrorism, not necessarily on personnel, Congressman.

Mr. ROHRABACHER. Well, personnel make policy, and if people are wrong to the point that thousands of Americans lost their lives, we, on this side of the branch of government, we in the legislative branch, have a right to know whether the personnel who were responsible for this were held accountable. And what I am suggesting is that the people at the State Department who were responsible for the policies that led to 9/11, some of them may still be in positions of authority, and that is what I am asking you. Were the people who were insisting before 9/11 that we work with the Taliban and undercutting the efforts, I might add, of those people who were trying to set up resistance to the Taliban, are those people still in positions of making decisions over at the State Department?

Mr. BLACK. I was not in the State Department then. I do not know.

Mr. ROHRABACHER. You have worked in the State Department, but you have not bothered to check to see——

Mr. BLACK. Congressman, I have not checked that question. On issues of 9/11,—this is meant to be a threat briefing on that—I am happy to talk about al-Qaeda, happy to talk about that.

Mr. ROHRABACHER. Obviously, this goes to where al-Qaeda came from.

Mr. BLACK. Yes, I know. If I could request, Mr. Chairman. I am scheduled to be in front of the 9/11 Committee on the 13th of April, so issues having to do with that, I would prefer to reserve for that. I am happy to talk about al-Qaeda and the terrorist threat, if I may, and I would like to leave other type topics like that to that time.

Mr. GALLEGLY. If Members would try to focus their energy on the al-Qaeda threat, that would be——

Mr. BLACK. I would appreciate it, Mr. Chairman. Thank you.

Mr. ROHRABACHER. Let me just note, you are a spokesman for the Administration, and you are here to testify. Mr. Chairman, I personally resent this Administration or any Administration not being willing to discuss the issues of importance at this level. This is how we learn. This is how we are going to do our job, and if we have people in this Administration or any other Administration who are refusing to talk about the people who actually made the decisions and whether or not they are still in decision-making positions, then if we are not insisting on those answers, we are not doing a job, and if you are not willing to tell us, you are not doing your job.

Mr. BLACK. Well, Congressman, I am trying to respond to you, sir, with the greatest of respect.

Mr. ROHRABACHER. All right.

Mr. BLACK. At that time, I was in the Central Intelligence Agency involved with that work. I was not in the State Department, and I was not involved in the decision-making process, and I was not intimately familiar with who was in what position making policy at the State Department. I did operational activities, and I produced intelligence.

Mr. ROHRABACHER. Might I suggest,——

Mr. BLACK. Yes, sir.

Mr. ROHRABACHER [continuing]. Having been in the Executive Branch myself,—I spent 7 years in the White House—might I suggest that you find out who amongst you in your group at the State Department now or who in the CIA was advocating those policies which led to this horrible tragedy that we suffered on 9/11 and not listen to their opinions or put them in other spots and be able to assure us that that happened?

When I was in the White House, we said, "People are policy." That is the first thing we learned. People were advocating certain things and were pushing certain things before 9/11, obviously, and I can tell you, I dealt with it before 9/11, obviously there were people pushing in exactly the wrong direction, which led to this catastrophe, and we need to know that has been cleaned up. Now, George Tenet is still director of the CIA, and as far as I am concerned, he should have been gone a long time ago.

The only assurance you can give us is to assure us that those people who were pushing the wrong policies are no longer in positions of making decisions, and I would hope we get that from this Administration. Thank you very much.

Mr. GALLEGLY. Mr. Schiff?

Mr. SHERMAN. Before Mr. Schiff speaks, I have a unanimous consent request that all Members be given up to 7 calendar days to furnish statements for the record.

Mr. GALLEGLY. Without objection. In fact, everyone that would like to submit a statement for the record should be given that opportunity, and we will, with unanimous consent, abide by the 7-day rule. Mr. Schiff?

Mr. SCHIFF. Thank you, Mr. Chairman.

Ambassador, I wanted to get your reaction to a quote attributed to an American official closely connected with counterterrorism. This was in a piece by Fareed Zakaria recently, where he quotes this official as saying that:

> "States have been getting out of the terror business since the late 1980s. We have kept many governments on the list of state sponsors for political reasons. The reality is that the terror we face is mostly unconnected with states."

Is that an accurate statement, not necessarily that they are on the list for political reasons, which is, obviously, a very pejorative connotation, but is the dominant threat we face right now not that of state-sponsored terrorism but, rather, local groups, loosely affiliated, if at all, but bonded by this common murderous ideology?

Mr. BLACK. Yes, sir. I think you are absolutely right. I think the trend is toward localized groups. I will say that the list of the state sponsors of terrorism is one that is very important to us. We look at it very closely. I would take exception that they are there for political reasons.

I do counterterrorism, and they are on it for specific reasons of counterterrorism. It is hard to get on this list, but it is also hard to get off, and there is a reason for it. We always look at ways when people meet our requirements. A country as an example that is making good progress is Sudan. They are going through the checklists. They have done a lot of good work. There are some areas that we are very concerned about still, such as——

Mr. SCHIFF. Ambassador, I do not need you to defend that particular point, which is the least interesting, from my point of view, but you do concur with the view that the predominant threat right now is not from states and their sponsorship but, rather, from these loosely affiliated, local organizations.

Mr. BLACK. I think the trend is in that direction. They are both dangerous. A state sponsor can utilize these groups to its own advantage. Their associations,—Iran and Hezbollah would be one example, but the trend is toward localized groups that are less connected.

Mr. SCHIFF. The state sponsorship may be critical in terms of the really potent terrorist weapons like a nuclear device or a radioactive device, et cetera, but if, then, the predominant threat today is these local groups that share this global ideology, the Bush doctrine is very general; it is more like a goal than an operational strategy.

Tell me, if you would, your view of what this ideology is that links these disparate groups of people because unless we have a clear understanding of the ideology, and we fight the ideology as well as those who carry the ideology, we are not going to be successful. It is obviously more than simple anti-Americanism because they are blowing up Saudis and Indonesians and fellow Muslims. It goes beyond those that have been working as allies in the war on terrorism. What is the essence of this ideology, and what is our strategy for going after it?

Mr. BLACK. The essence of the ideology, I think, is to overturn the trends of current events, to impose one's own vision of Islam and how society should be organized upon others. As an example, I think it is very instructive to look at the al-Qaeda organization, where, even before 9/11, you had isolated examples of maps of the world where they plan to have the whole planet—their favorite color is green—have it all go green. The objectives are comprehensive.

A part of this strategy to impose their will on others is the acceptance that this will be a long struggle, it will take a long time, and, to a certain extent, al-Qaeda's objective was to get this process in motion, to enlist others to their aid. There have been some aspects of our modern life that have facilitated this process—television, the Internet for forms of communication—to co-opt localized groups into the objective of overturning the establishment and to set up a brand of Islam that is extremely conservative and that is achieved by the use of terrorism.

Mr. SCHIFF. What is our strategy to combat the ideology? And given how unpopular we are around the world right now, doesn't that pose a real problem for us in essentially the propaganda war that is going on? How can we be successful when much of the world has such a violent animosity toward the United States right now?

Mr. BLACK. This strategy is based upon empowering the international community, build a coalition of nations, first of all, to conduct those law enforcement, intelligence, and legal activities to protect innocent people from attack. And then to go beyond that, if you are looking at underlying causes, we do have a lot of work to do there to get out a message. Even in the State Department, we have a new assistant secretary, Margaret Tutweiler, who is looking at the public diplomacy aspects. These are areas that we are looking at and need to do a better job of to get our message out.

Mr. SCHIFF. Thank you, Ambassador.

Mr. GALLEGLY. Mr. King?

Mr. KING. Thank you, Mr. Chairman.

Ambassador Black, I want to commend you for the terrific job you have done for our country over the years. I realize there are limitations on the specificity of answers you can give us, so I will be satisfied with a conceptual answer to the question I am going to try to pose to you.

If we are talking about 9/11, my understanding of Director Tenet's testimony was that, in the summer of 2001, almost all of the evidence was indicating, if there was going to be a spectacular attack, it would be overseas. Also, our domestic agencies were at the highest possible alert throughout the summer of 2001.

Richard Clarke said even if we had done everything he had wanted, it still would not have averted the September 11th attacks. Michael Sheehan, who I believe held a position similar to yours in the previous Administration and is presently doing an outstanding job in the New York Police Department, has said that no one could have anticipated the extent of the attacks of September 11th.

My concern with all of this is those attacks did happen. What are we doing now to think outside the box, to perhaps think diabolically, to anticipate—maybe the question answers itself—to anticipate something that otherwise we would not anticipate, either an attack against the United States or against American interests overseas because it looks as if whatever thinking we had, both the previous Administration and this Administration, prior to September 11th did not anticipate the extent, the enormity, and the horrific nature of the attacks of September 11th? Do you worry about there being something else out there that no one is thinking of now, and what are we doing to try to anticipate that?

Mr. BLACK. Yes. You are absolutely right. Do we worry about things? Do worry about things we have not thought of? Yes, all the time. I think a good sense of paranoia comes with this type of job.

This country is in a lot better shape now than it was before. Does this provide comprehensive assurance that nothing bad will happen? No. But when I compare and contrast what we had before with what we have now, it has greatly improved, and it is my professional view, Congressman, that these improvements have been instrumental in protecting this country.

On the one hand, you have an absolutely aggressive, go-get-them offense overseas, using partnerships with other countries, which is crucial. So that has attrited the capabilities of terrorist groups to project against American interests overseas but also against the

United States. So a good offense, a better offense, is what we have, and it is getting better all the time.

I know that the intelligence community has developed a new entity, the Terrorist Threat Integration Center, where all they do is look at what is the threat. This is a great advantage for people like me at the State Department because, in some circumstances in the past, you might have one view from the Defense Intelligence Agency, one view from intelligence at Treasury and across the board. Here, you have basically one conduit that provides me with the reality of what the threat is. This is a great, great thing. So we have sort of essentially one-stop shopping. They take all of the information. They collate it. They are in contact with their counterparts in other countries. They coordinate. They assess what is the threat, and they provide that to us, the customer. What is it we have to look for?

So more aggressive to collect information to disrupt overseas, both intelligence and law enforcement. The information, I think, is being handled in a more effective way that is of use to the consumer. A lot of it is also looked in terms of what is the impact on infrastructure. Hypothetically, if we get a report of terrorist interest in a bridge in your district or a type of bridge you have in your district, these people look at how hard is it to engage this target. What does it take to destroy a target like this? Experts take a look at this, come up with a fix, and they fix it and make it more secure. They do things like that, so there is a lot of red-teaming activity that goes into it.

The other thing is you have a Department of Homeland Security that has increased our awareness. The Transportation Security Administration—the checkers at the airport. What Homeland Security does, looking at all of the types of vulnerabilities, pulling the first responders together. We still have a ways to go, and some people kind of shake their head and say, "It is not perfect. I went through an airport somewhere, and they did not do that great a job."

But if you look at it from the standpoint of a terrorist attacking, their environment, if you think of trying to assault a castle, the wall is higher, the wall is thicker, you know, there are more people, they have got a rotweiler running in the front, and their attack plan is greatly complicated, and this is what I was trying to convey in another question.

If you are now put in the terrorist's situation, you have a much harder problem, which means you have got to go through your whole cycle again of pacing, figuring it all out, and then as they are doing that, we keep ratcheting up the defenses overseas, we keep being offensive, so if you do this right, you are degrading their ability to attack. Some will get through is probably a high probability, but maybe the analogy is air defense, concentric rings of defense. You degrade the strike so what gets closest to it needs to be protected. The homeland is something that can be handled and dealt with here.

Mr. KING. Thank you, Ambassador.

Mr. GALLEGLY. Ms. McCollum?

Ms. McCOLLUM. Thank you, Mr. Chair. Ambassador Black, thank you for being here today.

We keep talking about al-Qaeda, and we are here today to talk about al-Qaeda, but al-Qaeda is not a nation; it is ever evolving, as we all know. There are reports that it could be in anywhere up to 50 different countries. And my concern is, as we see the spread and the evolving of this, especially in light of what recently happened in Spain, we can start focusing on how to prevent attacks. We need to do that, and our Homeland Security is working on it, as well as the international community together, but we, in my opinion, have another challenge ahead of us, especially as al-Qaeda continues to evolve and spread and move out into different countries, and that is understanding the language and the culture.

As you so well put it, and as people say, and I will paraphrase, long haul, long time, long term, decades, this is going to be for the next generation, that we are going to have to keep working on destroying groups like al-Qaeda as they continue to evolve, working internationally, as well as keeping opportunities for al-Qaeda to come in and find recruits, the next generation of youth that are victimized into becoming suicide bombers.

So could you tell me what you are working on, if there are plans to capture not only people our age to start working and learning more about cultural sensitivities, those of us who have the ability to travel, people who are in the State Department who are involved in intelligence, to expand their knowledge of culture and language, and what we are doing or planning to do as a nation so that we have individuals with a diplomatic language and cultural skills so there are people who can pick up the nuances of what is in an e-mail or what has happened in a phone call or what they are hearing?

Mr. BLACK. Yes, ma'am. I would answer the question in two parts. One is that it is interesting for me to note, new immigrants to the United States from these very areas that we are interested in sometimes have such unique insights into the turn of a phrase or what a particular words means that you might not learn in school, so we have a great advantage, this being a melting pot and the people that naturally come in.

There is an across-the-board effort in the government, and I would have to research this and get back to you in writing to see if there are established programs and the like, but Congresswoman, I have been really impressed at the amount of time that people in the government, from the Secretary of State to Deputy Secretary Rich Armitage to all of the assistant secretaries, myself, people in the intelligence community, the time they spend working with young people, going out and talking to high school students, college students, giving lectures and underscoring those skills and traits that are sought for and desired in essentially this type of work.

And it is, I guess, sort of analogous to the days of the cold war, I guess, these days when you and I might remember learn Russian, see St. Petersburg, go through the Hermitage. We are trying to do this in areas now of interest to us that have great impact in counterterrorism. That is the good news. The bad news is there are a lot of countries that we are interested in, but the learning of languages is very important.

I think if you want to be successful in the field of counterterrorism, whether it is in the State Department or the intelligence community, you have got to learn, you have to know, a good language. This would be a key part of your career, whether it is Arabic or Farsi or Chinese. That is a prerequisite these days. We encourage people to know cultures, to travel.

The big change, in my view, is we are starting at a very young age, and because, as you underscored again, this is a long struggle. I know it will see me out. Perhaps it will also see you out. It is not going to go over quick. We are going to have to stick with it, and we are trying to build this infrastructure to reach out to kids to show them the great contribution they can make. It is not easy to encounter terrorism, but you can save lives, and they do seem to be attracted to it, so I think we are making progress in that area.

Ms. McCOLLUM. Mr. Chair, if I may, other State Department issues besides counterterrorism that are more in the diplomatic, hand-to-hand areas; do you know if there are programs being involved in there? I serve on the Education Committee, and I have not seen anything forthcoming from the Department of Education to really embrace and enhance and encourage learning more languages, learning about more cultures because Leave No Child Behind, with the high-risk, high-stakes testing, actually schools are cutting those programs.

Mr. BLACK. I would just have to say, what I am trying to report to you is the reality that I see from my position. If I may, I would have to go back and check. May I give you a written response? I am sure these programs have names, so we can give you the background to them.

Ms. McCOLLUM. Thank you, Mr. Chair, and I look forward to seeing that. Thank you, sir.

Mr. GALLEGLY. The gentleman from New Jersey, Mr. Chris Smith.

Mr. SMITH OF NEW JERSEY. Thank you very much, Mr. Chairman.

Ambassador Black, thank you for being a life saver. Thank you for dedicating 28 years of your life to protect Americans and our interests abroad. You have one of the most difficult portfolios, I think, at the State Department and the U.S. Government, and you should know everybody here deeply respects and are grateful for your work.

Mr. BLACK. I appreciate that. Thank you, Congressman.

Mr. SMITH OF NEW JERSEY. I do mean it.

Let me just ask you a couple of questions. At the 9/11 Commission hearing this month, former Secretary of State Madeline Albright said that the terrorist attack on our two Embassies in Africa, in Nairobi and Darisalam, which killed more than 300 people and wounded thousands more, was her worst day. You probably heard her say that. And, obviously, for many of us, it was a terrible, terrible day and the aftermath of that, which was the culmination of a number of incidents, going back to the Beirut bombing, in which one of my constituents, Paul Inasinze, was killed, a Marine, during that terrible tragedy.

On March 12, 1999, I chaired a hearing. I chaired the International Operations and Human Rights Committee for 6 years. We were putting together the State Department bill for that year, and we had a hearing on the security of U.S. missions abroad, and our principal witness was Admiral Crowe, as you know, the former Chairman of the Joint Chiefs of Staff and our Ambassador to the U.K. The Crowe Commission, which had these two accountability review boards that looked at those bombings, made some very, very troubling findings about what the status was in terms of our security.

Admiral Crowe said:

"There was a collective failure of the U.S. Government over the past decade . . ."

that would be the 1990s

". . . to provide adequate resources to reduce the vulnerability of U.S. diplomatic missions to terrorist attacks in most countries of the world."

Admiral Crowe pointed out, and this was his statement:

"The boards were most disturbed regarding two interconnected issues. The first was that there was an inadequacy of resources to provide security against terrorist attacks and, second, there was a relatively low priority accorded to security concerns throughout the U.S. Government by the Department of State and other agencies in general,"

and he said this was found in Washington as well as in the field. He also said that the Administration's request, at that time, was inadequate; it just was not enough.

My good friend, Mr. Delahunt, was at that hearing when we quizzed Admiral Crowe and others, and he made the point, rightfully so, that requests had been made for more money, but the Office of Management and Budget had intervened and said, no, you are not going to get it. We then forced the issue. I pushed my bill, which we dubbed the Embassies Security Act, to completion. It was signed into law as part of this overall State Department reauthorization. It had a lot of disparate elements, but that was the engine that drove it, and in the end, we got some, but I do not think all, of that money by the time we got to the appropriations process.

I guess my question is, you know, we have been hearing the blame game, which I, frankly, resent when I hear people talking about it because there is blame all around, but, frankly, when good people do all that they could possibly do, and OMB steps in, as they did then, and say you are not getting it, there is a problem, and our hearing highlighted that problem. I remember Dan Gensler from the Foreign Service Association,—he was the President—he made the point that we go from crisis to the next, and everybody is Johnny on the spot for the first year, and then it just falls off the table, and people are no longer as diligent.

I have not seen that in this Administration. I have not seen it over the last 3 years, and, believe me, I have followed it very, very closely.

My question to you would be about resources. Have we allocated sufficient resources to do the job? I would just say parenthetically, so many things may have led to 9/11, maybe not, but when I was in Berlin not so long ago as part of the OSC Parliamentary Assembly, which I chair, we heard from some people within the State Department, one of whom told me that in Bangladesh—this is just one little tidbit of information, but it plays into what really happened and what preceded the horrific events of 9/11—that on 31 occasions, people had gone to our Embassy or our consular in Bangladesh, had sought a visa, and their express purpose was for flight training. This was in the late 1990s. They were denied, every one of them.

They probably went somewhere else and eventually got it or got it under another pretext, but they had actually said flight training was why they wanted to come over here. And it did not ring any bells there, even though they were denied. There was no follow up here in Washington, and, in the end, those records were destroyed after a 2-year period, so we do not even know if Atta or anybody else were among those who were seeking that. So no bells went off, and that was in the 1990s, late 1990s.

But my question really goes to the adequacy of resources, if you could speak to that, because that was very serious. The first year after the bombing of our Embassies, $1.4 billion, as requested by Admiral Crowe, was provided like that. The next year, zero funding for 2000 for the very things that Admiral Crowe had agitated for and asked for.

Mr. BLACK. Yes, sir. If I may, I think you have a very valid point. If I may, I would like to give you a written response. That particular account would be done by diplomatic security. That would be Ambassador Frank Taylor, and he and I and Deputy Secretary Armitage would be eager to respond to.

As sort of an observer on Embassy security, I would tell you that I personally have always been so pleasantly surprised. The Secretary of State chairs a meeting at 8:30 in the morning, and I always sort of remember the amount of time spent on Embassy security, security overseas, how Embassies have been hardened, improvements that have been made, where we are planning to harden it. So I would tell you, as an observant of these types of activities, there is a tremendous emphasis on it. We do take it awfully seriously, again, because we know this is going to be for a long period of time that we have to keep this missions secure.

Mr. SMITH OF NEW JERSEY. If I could, Mr. Chairman, just very briefly follow up.

And the issue is not just hardening and setbacks and making sure that the glass is sufficiently protected so shards do not kill people if there is a bombing. The issue is also personnel so that the eyes and ears of the American government extend in that venue so that if there is a threat, we have an early warning device before it comes here because that is the outer reaches of U.S. interests.

Mr. BLACK. I do not know if this is in response to your question, but a program that we are very interested in is the Antiterrorism Assistance Program. We asked for a few monies, and we got less than we wanted. We think it is a good program, as well as our program of Terrorism Interdiction Program that was also cut. So I guess, in complete frankness, we did not get everything we asked for, but that is where we are, sir.

Mr. GALLEGLY. Nick Smith?

Mr. SMITH OF MICHIGAN. Thank you, Mr. Chairman.

It appears that there are thousands, if not hundreds of thousands, of Islamic extremists that wake up every morning trying to think of ways that they can kill or damage Americans or the West, so I appreciate your comment that we cannot totally protect ourselves when we have got that kind of an attitude and that kind of determination to damage us.

I would like to get your reaction to what happened yesterday or the day before in Fallujah, where the four Americans were tortured, beaten, burned, stomped on during their burning, and the cheering crowds around. Two questions. One, what is the relation with al-Qaeda? But first of all, help me better understand the kind of attitude that seems so inconceivable to most of us that a crowd can gather around and cheer with that kind of, for lack of a better word, brutality.

Mr. BLACK. Yes, sir. I cannot tell you how sad we all are to see that, and this takes me back. I have seen these things before.

Mr. SMITH OF MICHIGAN. Specifically, is there still training in Muslim teachings that can excite individuals to be that terrorist? And I suspect that there must be. What is the attitude? Of course, it is in the area where they are vulnerable.

Mr. BLACK. If you are looking at this particular case, you have a population that is generally pretty hostile to the United States, and this is the Fallujah area. This is basically the base of the people that were doing well with the Saddam Hussein regime. By this new dispensation, this new change, the Coalition's facilitation of a drive toward democracy, they have everything to lose and nothing to gain. They are fighting for a way of life that they have lost.

Mr. SMITH OF MICHIGAN. Just so my 5 minutes do not go totally by——

Mr. BLACK. I am sorry. I want to try to answer your question.

Mr. SMITH OF MICHIGAN. These young people—it appears from the newspaper articles that they are fairly young, under 20—that are cheering.

Mr. BLACK. I think since it specifically happened in the Fallujah area, which is very Saddam Hussein oriented, tribally oriented, they do see us as the enemy, and their natural inclination until we prove them otherwise is to vent their frustration, what they see as their humiliation and defeat against an outside force, against representatives of that entity. It is not that uncommon.

Mr. SMITH OF MICHIGAN. Would there be indications, or do we have information, that the Islamic fundamental interpretation of the Koran is still being taught in the area, and that is part of the reason?

Mr. BLACK. The last reports that I have read on this particular subject in this area is that in that particular area there is a proportionately high number of mosques that are being very anti-Coalition, anti-American, but they are usually quite adept at stopping just short of espousing violence against Americans.

So you can look at that in two different ways. One is legitimate expression stopping short of violence, or you can see this as sort of code words to go forth and wreak violence. The people that did this were not, you know, three guys on an excellent adventure. These are people that have had the training, have a vested interest——

Mr. SMITH OF MICHIGAN. People that were stomping on those burned bodies.

Mr. BLACK. Those would be sort of people standing by.

Mr. SMITH OF MICHIGAN. Let me just ask you to finish up on any relationship you see between al-Qaeda and that kind of Islamic terrorism that is taking place.

Mr. BLACK. From our perspective, it is associated. It is in proximity. There is not specifically a direct tie between that crowd and al-Qaeda as we know it. They just find themselves, the enemy of my enemy is my friend.

Mr. GALLEGLY. Ms. Watson?

Ms. WATSON. Thank you, Mr. Ambassador, for being here in the tough situation that we face, and I have a multipart question, so let me go through my statement and question, and then any piece of it you would like to respond to, I would appreciate it.

There is concern that the terrorist organizations are trading in African natural resources as a means of screening and moving their financial assets, and it is reported that Charles Taylor, when he was President of Liberia, from al-Qaeda's trade in West African diamonds, was part of this network. On Tuesday, your colleague at the Treasury Department, William Fox, the head of the Treasury's Financial Crimes Enforcement Network, told a meeting of the World Diamond Council in Dabai that the industry was vulnerable to abuse by criminals and terrorists. He is reported to have said:

> "Although evidence to prove the connections between diamonds and terrorists is still being developed, we are receiving enough information from government agencies, private concerns, and the industry to warrant a closer examination of the problem."

And I would like to know what you might know or what you might tell us about these connections, and what is your office doing to undermine the source of funding that allows al-Qaeda to come into Iraq and do the kinds of dastardly deeds that were just done?

The General Accounting Office said late last year that diamonds and other commodities could be used to earn, move, or store terrorist assets but said the extent of the business was unknown, in part because the U.S. Government had failed to collect information about the problem systematically.

So if you can, would you let us know if your office has made any effort to investigate and collect data on this problem, and if not, why not because it is obvious that there is a great amount of funds out there being used by al-Qaeda and Osama bin Laden, and I think that the diamond trade might be part of that. So if you can respond, I would appreciate it.

Mr. BLACK. Yes, ma'am. I will try. I think this would stem from a couple of points, if I may. The first thing is it generally does not take a lot of money to conduct a terrorist operation, comparatively, a lot less than we would naturally think. So generally, you are not involving large sums of money.

We have an active program that seeks to identify and to cut financial links to terrorists. As a result of this, we have frozen more than $130 million around the world of monies associated with terrorist groups. In some countries, like Saudi Arabia, we look, particularly, at funding from potential charities to terrorist groups and seek to cut that and identify it.

As we are more effective in cutting off the established financial links to terrorist groups,—wire transfers to banks, things like that—it is only natural to assume that terrorists will seek other ways to move monies to support their training and their operations. The African piece, in particular, whether they are talking about emeralds out of the Copper Belt in Zambia or diamonds out of the Democratic Republic of Congo, Liberia, there are other associations with this that, in my mind, take precedence over, particularly, use for terrorism. Yes, it is a possibility. It is something that we need to look at closely. It is generally associated more with established criminal activities or smuggling activities.

So it is something that needs to be looked at. We have to look at any new form terrorists may hijack to move resources and money, but that would go well beyond, I think, ma'am, hard gems. It can go to anything that has value that they would attempt to escape our scrutiny and to reach their operatives. So I would agree with Mr. Fox. This is something that deserves close attention.

I will say, my recollection is efforts to investigate these kinds of things in the past have not supported the contention that terrorists, at least the terrorists that we are looking at, al-Qaeda and their associates, have been associated with this trade, with using hard gems as a vehicle from the source. We are looking at all of these avenues.

There is a tremendous infrastructure, certainly in counterterrorism, but there are lots of people and organizations and computers and everything that look at how terrorists move money. This was a cornerstone, certainly, of this Administration—"to drain the swamp" is the phrase that they always use—to look at these links to try to keep money away from them, and it is complex.

One of the things that have been used where we are also making progress in shutting down are jawalas, which is the informal transfer mechanism. Basically, if you are in California, and I am somewhere else, I call you. I make a deposit at my end, you make a deposit at yours, and it obviates classical financial communications.

So we are looking at all of this, being mindful of the fact that as we make progress to shut down one medium, like criminals or crooks, they will find another way to do it, and the trick is just to get ahead of these people.

Ms. WATSON. In the time I have left, Mr. Chair, I would like to make this——

Mr. GALLEGLY. The gentlelady's time has expired, so if you would make it brief, I would allow just a brief question.

Ms. WATSON. Yes. As you relate to other questions that will be asked here, who is the enemy? How do we get to them? So that is why I asked that question. I know they are operating in other places around the world. We talk about al-Qaeda. Where are they? How will we get to them? How will we hold them responsible for those acts that are committed? Thank you very much, Mr. Chairman.

Mr. BLACK. Is it all right to respond to that, sir?

Mr. GALLEGLY. Yes, if you would like.

Mr. BLACK. The question of who we are dealing with has evolved over time. I can remember the beginnings of the al-Qaeda organization in Khartoum, Sudan. They developed lines of communication, infrastructure. They matured into an organization that had lines of communications out to other like-minded people. The people that we are looking at are the ones who feel there is a lot of psychology involved in this. There is a lot of victimization, where trusted elders basically entrap young people into this and encourage it. There is a production line, essentially, to sensitize young people into a cause, into a way of life, but it is based, I think, on feeling some psychological aspects having to do with the family, aspects of humiliation, wanting to wreak revenge, a throwback to history when their society was more predictable, more understandable. It is a drive for conservatism, and there is a drive to overturn what is an established path of history.

It is quite a trick, I think, to take a young person, and now it has even turned to young women who are prepared to leave their young children to become suicide attackers. There has also been, in my view, a failure of moderate leaders in these countries to stand up, to speak reason, to describe what is right and what is wrong, and to work with their own populations to provide them the opportunities they need so that they feel comfortable in their own societies. So we are having to make up for quite a bit.

I think the first step, certainly, which is ongoing, is to identify and stop those that are trying to kill us and to kill our families, is the first step, and the second is working with our partners around the world to come up with societies that facilitate and allow freedom of expression and that take away feelings of humiliation, lack of power and who confront the radical terrorist leaders that bring these young people into this cause.

I am very confident we will win; their cause is so misguided and crazy, from our standpoint. But unfortunately, this is going to take time, it is going to take effort, and I think, as the President has said, we have to have determination and stick with this, and I think, with the passage of time, we will all be safe, but it will be quite the struggle.

Mr. GALLEGLY. The gentleman from Indiana, Mr. Pence.

Mr. PENCE. Thank you, Chairman, and thank you, Mr. Ambassador, for your testimony today.

First, just a follow-up question. In your earlier testimony, you mentioned, in passing, that we have frozen about $130 million in assets around the world. Can you speak to the degree to which those are assets associated with Osama bin Laden or his family? To what degree have we frozen his assets?

Mr. BLACK. I would have to give you a written breakdown. I am just not prepared, at this point, to give which particular group, but this is across the spectrum of assets, terrorist assets, and not just the al-Qaeda organization. A goodly amount of this, and, again, I have to apologize—I am going to have to give you a written response—a good percentage of this has been conducted overseas by our partners in freezing funds overseas, so this is the aggregate total.

So I think that is good, but the other point is that we are making progress, particularly in countries like Saudi Arabia, where the funding mechanisms are being looked at very carefully. A charity is now only allowed to have one bank account. Those in Saudi Arabia that wish to make contributions, say, to refugees in Iraq have to do it in kind, not with cash. Saudis are no longer allowed to contribute cash to the cash box in mosques and in public places that used to exist to collect funds. They are concerned about the diversion of these things. They have all been removed. There are established, controlled mechanisms that are subject to audit, and we all have ways to look at this. We do look at it to make sure these monies go for good works.

So I guess I would say, Congressman, there is a system. At the beginning, people always think about how great the problem, a big problem. At least, we have started, and we are on the right road.

Mr. PENCE. I sense, then, an affirmative response that some of the assets may be assets of Osama bin Laden.

Mr. BLACK. Yes, sir.

Mr. PENCE. I have some memory of press accounts of a billion dollars in personal resources that may be associated with him or available to him, and most of my constituents would think that tying up his money would be a very important aspect.

Mr. BLACK. Correct. I would say, if I could just interject,——

Mr. PENCE. Please.

Mr. BLACK [continuing]. We do know from intelligence that their operational people, their cells, are having extreme problems trying to access funds, trying to get money. These guys are under real stress, and they are in needs of even small infusions of new monies. So we are making progress. We have had impact. We have a lot more to do, but we are getting there.

Mr. PENCE. A good sign.

Let me go next, then, to—I was very interested in some of your reflections on Osama bin Laden and his possible leadership role in al-Qaeda. What is your sense? I know that your prepared summary suggests that the jury is out as to whether or not Osama bin Laden is still continuing to lead this organization. Forgive me if you have already responded.

Mr. BLACK. No, I have not.

Mr. PENCE. Is he still in charge of al-Qaeda, in the judgment of the State Department?

Mr. BLACK. That is a good way to put it, and I think it is reflective of the larger intelligence community, but, again, for a real definitive view, you would probably want to access them. They would be happy to provide that information to you. But, you know, the sense is that he is not leader in the way we think of it, a leader who is in control, holds meetings with his lieutenants, communicates with his subordinates, receives information, validates plans, and allocates resources. No. This guy spends most of his time trying to figure out, you know, how they are going to come for me, and is this going to be the day?

With that in mind, there are elements of communication he maintains in contact, but I think the development is that command and control has decentralized to others. We would probably have the same system if this country was under a catastrophic, classical, military attack. Subordinate commanders would assume control, and you are seeing that in a very loose way.

Mr. PENCE. Which gives evidence of the fact that, through a variety of countermeasures, his leadership has been largely neutralized over al-Qaeda.

Mr. BLACK. Yes. The impact, his effectiveness, has been greatly reduced, yes, sir.

Mr. PENCE. Thank you, Ambassador.

That is all I have, Mr. Chairman.

Mr. GALLEGLY. Thank you, Mr. Pence. Without objection, the Chair would recognize the gentleman from Massachusetts, Mr. Delahunt.

Mr. DELAHUNT. I want to join Mr. Smith's observations about your contribution, Mr. Ambassador. Thank you for what you do, and you do it extremely well. And I think this has been an excellent hearing. I think you have educated us, and as a segue to Mr. Pence, I, on my own, just from the readings I have done, I have reached a conclusion, too, that Osama bin Laden, at this point, is more of a symbol than an actual CEO, albeit it is still important, because symbols are important, it is obviously important to either capture him or kill him.

But the concern that I have, all of us, the American people, Members of Congress, those that do not deal with it on an every day basis is this: The focus is so discreet on al-Qaeda that I am concerned that there is a sense that if al-Qaeda is defeated, terrorism is going away. My own observation is that as al-Qaeda wanes in the era of terrorism, these smaller, localized, regional groups, in fact, are growing, for whatever reason, and I do not want to get into that today. But am I on the right track when I make that comment?

Mr. BLACK. I think you are absolutely correct.

Mr. DELAHUNT. Let me ask you this, and I thought what your testimony was particularly important on this point: I think we have really got to define the enemy today. There are multiple terrorist groups all over the world, some of which really do not pose a threat to the United States, and that is our concern. It is a concern that has to be our priority, albeit we are concerned about terrorism in general.

I think you stated earlier that the nexus of these groups are their shared corrupted version of a great religion. The states that are currently on the terrorist list put out by DOS, the state sponsors of terrorism, on that list, which of those states are harboring, protecting, or supporting that particular group of organizations, however loosely organized they may be?

I am trying to think of who is on the state-sponsors-of-terrorism list, but could you run through them for us?

Mr. BLACK. I will try, and I hope I do not leave any out. If you begin with Iran, here you have a country that has been on the list a long time. There is no doubt about it that they are a state sponsor of terrorism. They actively support Hezbollah, a validated foreign terrorist organization, with funds, support, information, training.

Mr. DELAHUNT. Let me just interrupt because I know time is quick.

Mr. BLACK. I am sorry. I could go on. I am glad you cut me off.

Mr. DELAHUNT. Right. But Hezbollah, for example; do they share this corrupted version of Islam?

Mr. BLACK. This really gets sort of in a philosophical point. Hezbollah's drive is the relentless overturning of the State of Israel.

Mr. DELAHUNT. Let me just run through them. My aide just gave me the list.

North Korea does not harbor any of these particular terrorist groups.

Mr. BLACK. Not that I am aware of. It is more their propensity for and actions in the past. One of the most important of these, of course, is the hostages from Japan. I want to mention that.

Mr. DELAHUNT. I am not questioning the list itself, but about the enemy, this enemy that attacked us. Cuba?

Mr. BLACK. Their past actions and their performance.

Mr. DELAHUNT. Libya?

Mr. BLACK. Libya making dramatic changes. They retain some contacts with terrorist groups we are concerned about, but we are working with them to resolve that.

Mr. DELAHUNT. Syria?

Mr. BLACK. Syria in contact with everybody, providing aid, comfort, and support to a spectrum of terrorist organizations.

Mr. DELAHUNT. Sudan?

Mr. BLACK. Sudan, great progress, assisting in the global war on terrorism, but they so far have not expelled offices of the Palestinian Islamic Jihad and Hamas, which we have instructed them they must do.

Mr. DELAHUNT. So Iran and Syria, in terms, again, of these not secular terrorists but these fundamental Islamist terrorists. Syria and Iran?

Mr. BLACK. Syria and Iran are very high on this list, yes, Congressman.

Mr. GALLEGLY. I want to thank the Members for their participation today, and I would just like to say to you, Mr. Ambassador, that we all have concerns and questions about some of the operations of our intelligence gathering over years and months past, and certainly I understand Mr. Rohrabacher's concerns and identify with some of them.

But I want to make it very clear that I want to associate myself with the comments of Mr. Chris Smith of New Jersey and Mr. Delahunt regarding the job you have done, the candor you have provided to this Committee, and the growing relationship that we have personally established, and I want to thank you for the 28-plus years of service you have had and for the tremendous contribution that you make to this Committee, and with that, the Subcommittee stands adjourned.

[Whereupon, at 11:19 a.m., the Subcommittee was adjourned.]

○